12 Short Hikes
NEAR KEENE VALLEY

BY PHIL BROWN & TOM WOODMAN

Photos by Nancie Battaglia
Maps by Nancy Bernstein

 An ADIRONDACK EXPLORER Guidebook

Giant's Washbowl sits high above Chapel Pond Pass.

Published by
ADIRONDACK EXPLORER
36 Church Street, Saranac Lake, NY 12983
AdirondackExplorer.org
&
LOST POND PRESS
Saranac Lake, NY
LostPondPress.com

Cover Photo: Noonmark Mountain, by Nancie Battaglia
Back Cover Photo: Nun-da-ga-o Ridge, by Phil Brown
Book Design: Susan Bibeau

ISBN: 978-0-9903090-3-1

Foreword

We at the *Adirondack Explorer* believe that the Adirondack Park is one of the most beautiful places on the planet. That's why our newsmagazine focuses on ways to protect and enjoy it. We hope this guidebook will lead to adventures that will enhance your appreciation of this marvelous place.

Although Tom Woodman and I wrote the book, many others had a hand in its production. Susan Bibeau designed the covers and inside pages. Nancy Bernstein drew all the maps by hand. Nancie Battaglia contributed breathtaking photographs. Tom and I want to thank two members of the *Explorer* staff—Associate Publisher Betsy Dirnberger, and writer Mike Lynch—for reading our copy, catching mistakes, and offering helpful suggestions. For various other contributions, we are grateful to two other *Explorer* staffers, Michael Armstrong and Andreas Mowka, and to the publication's founder, Dick Beamish.

The *Explorer* is very grateful to Annette Merle-Smith for her underwriting of this publication.

If you're unfamiliar with the *Explorer*, please take the time to check it out. We are a nonprofit newsmagazine that publishes six issues a year in addition to an annual Outings Guide. For Adirondack aficionados, it is essential reading. Find out more at **AdirondackExplorer.org**.

Enjoy the hikes!

—Phil Brown

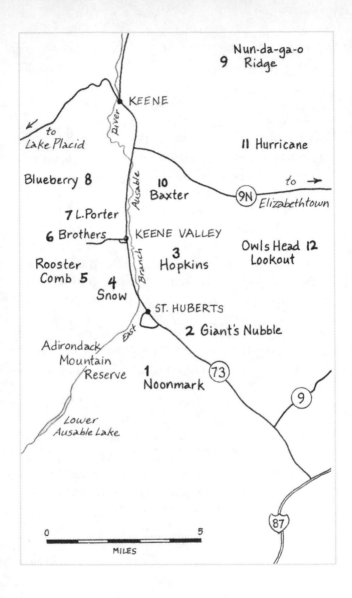

CONTENTS:

Introduction

Keene Valley is the home of the High Peaks. From here and the nearby communities of Keene and St. Huberts, tens of thousands of visitors each year begin hikes into rugged wilderness with the aim of climbing one or more of the tallest mountains in the state. Not only do the High Peaks pose a physical challenge, but they also offer the Adirondack Park's most dramatic scenery: views of slide-scarred slopes, deep valleys, and vast expanses of unbroken forest.

Sometimes, though, the challenge might be too much. If you're looking for a short hike—one that won't take all day or overexert the kids—Keene Valley has plenty of smaller peaks and lookouts with views comparable to those from loftier summits.

12 Short Hikes Near Keene Valley is the third in a series of guidebooks created by the *Adirondack Explorer*, a nonprofit newsmagazine with a strong interest in outdoor recreation and environmental issues. Publisher Tom Woodman and Editor Phil Brown teamed up to describe a dozen of the best short hikes in the region.

Given the steepness of the terrain around Keene Valley, the hikes are, on average, more arduous than those in the *Explorer*'s earlier two books. Nevertheless, most of the hikes can be done in four hours or less. In some cases, the authors suggest options to shorten an outing by, for example, turning around at a lookout rather than the summit.

Each chapter includes clear driving directions and GPS co-ordinates to get you to the trailhead as well as a statistical over-view (distance, elevation gain, etc.) to allow you to gauge the difficulty of the hike. The descriptions of the hikes are concise but informative. Historical tidbits enliven your interest in an outing. The trails are shown in the distinctive hand-drawn maps of Nancy Bernstein, a local artist. Photos were contributed by one of the Park's best photographers, Nancie Battaglia.

Although these are short hikes, don't take them lightly. Whenever you enter the wilderness, you should be prepared in case someone turns an ankle or worse. This means carrying the Ten Essentials. The classic list is as follows: topo map, compass, sunglasses and sunscreen, extra clothing, headlamp or flashlight, first-aid kit, fire-starter, matches, knife, and extra food. It's also wise to carry an emergency shelter such as a space blanket, a lightweight tent, or just a large trash bag. If you have a cell phone, bring it for emergencies, but be aware that it may not pick up a signal in the wild.

These hikes are largely in the Forest Preserve, public land protected by the state constitution as "forever wild." Ten of the hikes (Hurricane Mountain and Nun-da-ga-o Ridge are exceptions) take place in the High Peaks Wilderness, Dix Mountain Wilderness, or Giant Mountain Wilderness. Groups in these Wilderness Areas are limited to eight hikers, and dogs must be kept on leashes on trails. In some cases, a trail may cross private property. If so, do not stray from the route. Whether you're in the Forest Preserve or on private property, respect the land. Leave it as you found it.

The Adirondack Park contains 2.6 million acres of Forest Preserve, with thousands of miles of trails. We hope hiking the trails in this book will inspire you to discover more of the Adirondacks. If so, you should consider joining the Adirondack Mountain Club (ADK) and subscribing to the *Adirondack Explorer*. Information about both can be found on their websites: ADK.org and AdirondackExplorer.org.

And if you are venturing into other parts of the Park, you may want to pick up *12 Short Hikes Near Lake Placid* and *12 Short Hikes Near Old Forge*.

The state Department of Environmental Conservation's emergency hotline is 518-891-0235.

How hard is that hike?

In gauging the difficulty of a hike, two major consider-ations are its length and elevation gain. In our statistical over-views, provided at the head of each chapter, we indicate the distance of the hike (in miles) and the overall ascent (in feet). These figures are used to calculate the average grade from the trailhead to the summit or high point. The exception is Nun-da-ga-o Ridge. Because this loop is undulating, we used the sum of the elevation gains to calculate the average grade. The first three lists can be used to compare the relative difficulty of the hikes.

The two short lists are our rankings of the easiest and most scenic hikes. Since all of the hikes in the book offer wonderful views, the latter list is especially subjective

ROUND TRIP IN MILES
1. Baxter 2.6
2. First Brother 3.0
3. Snow 3.4
4. Little Porter 3.8
5. Noonmark 4.7
6. Rooster Comb 4.8
7. Blueberry 4.8
8. Owl Head Lookout 5.2
9. Giant's Nubble 5.4
10. Nun-da-ga-o 6.0
11. Hopkins 6.4
12. Hurricane 6.6

ELEVATION GAIN IN FEET
1. Baxter 770
2. Little Porter 1,200
3. Snow 1,360
4. Owl Head Lookout 1,430
5. First Brother 1,435
6. Giant's Nubble 1,480
7. Nun-da-ga-o 1,500
8. Rooster Comb 1,750
9. Hurricane 2,040
10. Hopkins 2,120
11. Blueberry 2,225
12. Noonmark 2,250

Noonmark has a spectacular view of the Great Range.

AVERAGE GRADE (%)
1. Nun-da-ga-o 8.1
2. Owl Head Lookout 10.4
3. Baxter 11.2
4. Hurricane 11.7
5. Little Porter 12.0
6. Hopkins 12.5
7. Rooster Comb 13.8
8. Giant's Nubble 14.0
9. Snow 15.2
10. Blueberry 17.9
11. First Brother 18.1
12. Noonmark 18.5

EASIEST
1. Baxter
2. Little Porter
3. Owl Head Lookout
4. Snow
5. Giant's Nubble

MOST SCENIC
1. Noonmark
2. First Brother
3. Nun-da-ga-o
4. Hurricane
5. Hopkins

1 Noonmark Mountain

Distance: 4.7 miles round trip
Elevation: 3,556 feet
Elevation gain: 2,250 feet
Average grade: 18.5%
Trailhead coordinates: N 44° 08.993′, W 73° 46.069′

Both Noonmark and neighboring Round Mountain boast open summits with excellent views of the High Peaks. Which to climb? The hike to Round is a bit easier, but Noonmark is the taller peak with somewhat better views. If you can't decide, you can combine the two in a 7-mile loop.

We'll describe only the hike to Noonmark in detail. Since there are many views on the way up, you could shorten the hike by turning around at a lookout below the summit.

> Noonmark Mountain lies due south of Keene Valley, so when the sun is directly above the summit, it is said to mark noon.

Don't be too daunted by the round-trip mileage. The hike's first half-mile or so is on roads, so you are on a trail for only 3.6 miles. But they are tough miles: this is the steepest hike in the book and entails some scrambling over bare rock.

The hike begins on property owned by the Ausable Club. You are not allowed to leave the trail until reaching public land. From the parking area, walk up Ausable Road. In a tenth of a mile, you pass the trailhead for Round Mountain (2.3 miles to the summit). A third of a mile up the road, you come to

With its slide scars, Dix Mountain looks as if it were clawed by a panther.

the Noonmark register on the left at the start of a driveway. For simplicity's sake, we measured trail mileages from the register.

Walk up the driveway for 0.2 miles, then turn right onto the trail. You pass through a hemlock grove, with a ravine on the left below you. At 0.4 miles, the trail crosses a stream on boulders and begins to steepen. It soon reaches a junction with the Old Dix Trail, by which time you are in the Forest Preserve.

Bear right at the signpost. The trail continues to ascend, sometimes moderately, sometimes steeply. At 1.0 mile, it bends right at the base of a small cliff and scrambles up to a ledge with the first vista. You can see Giant Mountain to the northeast and many of the High Peaks in the Great Range to the west. The Ausable Club and its golf course are below.

The trail re-enters the woods and then scampers over a bedrock outcrop. Turn around for a good view of Roaring Brook Falls spilling down the lower slope of Giant. As you ascend, you begin to glimpse Round Mountain through the trees on the left.

At 1.4 miles, you reach another lookout with a view of the Great Range. Soon after, you come to a view of Giant and Round. At 1.6 miles, you climb a small rustic ladder. More vistas follow. At 1.7 miles, you can see the top of Noonmark looming above.

After climbing another ladder, you enjoy numerous other views, each seemingly better than the one before. Finally, at 2.0 miles, you arrive at the open summit, with a breathtaking panorama that includes a knockout view of Dix Mountain, its flanks scarred by white bedrock as if it had been clawed by a panther. The vista also includes the Great Range, Mount Marcy, Giant, and much more.

If doing a round trip, retrace your steps and take in all the views again on the way down. If doing the loop, go over the summit and descend the other side of Noonmark (often steeply) for 1.0 mile to the Old Dix Trail. Turn left and go 0.6 miles to a junction. The trail to the right climbs 0.7 miles to the summit of Round.

–PB

DIRECTIONS: From the bridge over Johns Brook (near the Mountaineer), drive south on NY 73 for 3.3 miles to Ausable Road on the right. As soon as you turn, you'll see the public parking area on the left. (Note that this is the southern end of Ausable Road. On the way to the trailhead, you pass the northern end in St. Huberts.) If you're coming from the south, the turn will be on the left 5.3 miles past the intersection of US 9 and NY 73.

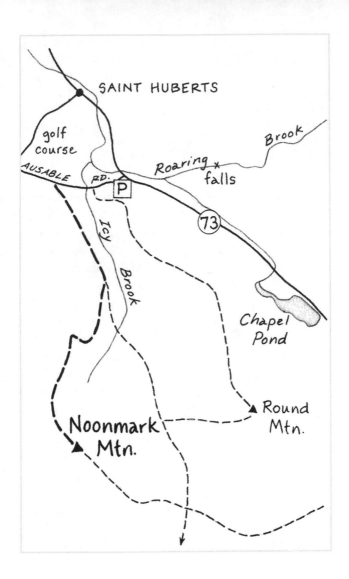

2 Giant's Nubble

Distance: 5.4 miles semi-loop
Elevation: 2,760 feet
Elevation gain: 1,480
Average grade: 14%
Trailhead coordinates: N 44° 09.018', W 073° 46.024'

This 5.4-mile hike combines close-up views of Roaring Brook Falls (from its top and bottom) with a striking vista from the Nubble, followed by a visit to Giant's Washbowl, a secluded high-elevation pond. Those who don't want an extended outing can turn around after visiting the falls. The hike also can be shortened by doing a round trip to the Nubble and skipping the Washbowl.

The trail begins as a wide, level path leading from the end of a parking area off Route 73 and along the bank of Roaring Brook. At 0.1 miles a side trail branches off to the right and brings you to the bottom of the falls in a quarter-mile of easy walking. The brook lives up to its name here as it roars through a cleft in a rock face and drops about 100 feet to the base. In all, Roaring Brook Falls drops in stages about 300 feet, qualifying it as one of the tallest cascades in the Adirondacks. If you step back far enough from the base, you can see the top of the falls.

In 1963, Roaring Brook Falls disappeared temporarily as a massive landslide diverted the water into Putnam Brook. Conservation officers built dikes to restore the flow.

Back at the junction, the main trail starts to climb gradually and then steepens moderately as it swings away from

Giant's Nubble attracts hikers of all ages.

the falls. At 0.5 miles from the trailhead a short side trail to the right passes through a camping area to the top of the falls, where gentle rapids lead to the cataract below. Wide bedrock ledges provide views of Noonmark Mountain and the peaks of the lower Great Range. Use care at the overlook as there have been tragic cases of hikers falling.

Returning to the trail and turning right, you reach a brook crossing at 1.2 miles. In high water, you may need to ford the narrow waterway, but it is not a significant obstacle. Just past the brook, you come to a junction. The trail to the summit of Giant Mountain goes left. You want to go straight. In 0.2 miles, you arrive at another junction, the start of a 2.6-mile loop (including a short side trip to the Nubble lookout). We'll describe a clockwise trip, ascending to the Nubble and returning via Washbowl Pond.

Bearing left at the junction, climb steadily for 0.8 miles to a small sign pointing to the Nubble (2.1 miles from the trailhead). Turn right to clamber over a ledge and walk out onto open rocks. A path through scrub leads to a rock outcropping with wide views to the south. The Ausable Club golf course and clubhouse sit at the base of the Great Range. Behind you, to the northeast, is a good view of the slides of Giant. To the left, Round Mountain and Noonmark rise in the foreground with the Dix Range beyond.

After returning to the main trail, turn right to continue the clockwise loop. The 0.7-mile descent to the Washbowl begins steeply but soon eases. At 0.2 miles from the Nubble, you can look down on the small pond encircled by thick forest, with the rock cliffs near Chapel Pond rising in the distance. Soon afterward, you reach a junction with the Ridge Trail leading to Giant's summit. Turn right here and continue descending. In another 0.2 miles, the trail crosses a brook and comes to the shore of the Washbowl.

Cross a plank bridge and bear right at the next junction. The trail follows the southern shore of the pond, with views of the Nubble and cliffs above the opposite shore. The descent back to the Roaring Brook Falls Trail is moderately pitched. From here, retrace your route back to the parking lot.

–TW

DIRECTIONS: From the Johns Brook bridge in Keene Valley (near the Mountaineer), drive south on NY 73 for 3.3 miles to the Roaring Brook parking area on the left. If coming from the south, the parking area is 5.3 miles past the intersection of US 9 and NY 73.

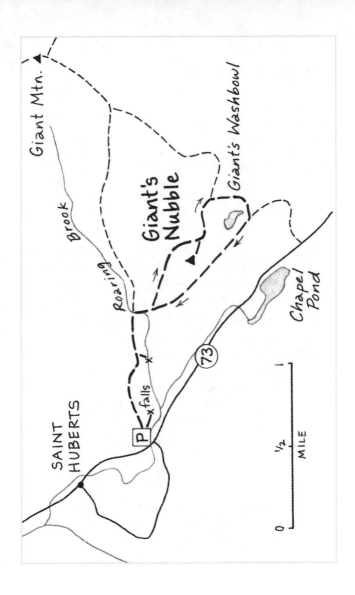

3 Hopkins Mountain

Distance: 6.4 miles round trip
Elevation: 3,183 feet
Elevation gain: 2,120 feet
Average grade: 12.5%
Trailhead coordinates: N 44° 09.767', W 073° 46.637'

The Mossy Cascade Trail to Hopkins Mountain offers a half-day excursion with spectacular views from the summit. For those who'd like a shorter hike, the Mossy Cascade waterfall can be reached in an easy three-quarter-mile walk.

While much of the 3.2-mile ascent to the summit is on moderate terrain with even footing, there are steep stretches, and the final push is over steep and rugged terrain. The payoff is a view of greater than 180 degrees that includes Giant Mountain, Dix, Sawteeth and the Great Range. The clubhouse and golf course of the Ausable Club stand out at the foot of the vast green wilderness in front of you.

> Hopkins Mountain was named for the Reverend Erastus Hopkins, a Troy minister and contemporary of nineteenth-century guide Old Mountain Phelps.

Parking for the trailhead is a pull-out on Route 73 near the south end of a bridge over the East Branch of the Ausable River. The trail, marked by red disks, leads past a guardrail and across a bridge over a small tributary of the East Branch. Walking along a bank overlooking the river, you arrive at a house on the left at 0.4 miles. At this point the trail joins a dirt road and then almost immediately swings

Hopkins's open summit offers a fantastic vista.

left off the road onto a more overgrown road.

After a half-mile of mostly level walking you encounter Mossy Cascade Brook. Walking along the stream, you can enjoy the white turbulence and musical splash of the brook dropping gently over a series of ledges. At 0.7 miles you see a sign for Hopkins and Giant.

Stay on the trail as it becomes moderately steep and switchbacks up the hillside. Along the way, paths have been worn in to provide glimpses of the rapids below. The bank above the brook falls off steeply, so be cautious.

Near the top of this short climb, just after a small set of wooden steps on the trail, you come to a fine view of the falls through the trees just off the trail to the left.

The trail climbs moderately from here. A mile from the trailhead you can see a clearing and home through the trees on the right. The trail crosses the brook here, and the rock-hopping can be tricky in high water. The upward journey continues in moderately steep pitches alternating with level stretches. At one point, the trail descends into a hollow, but don't be fooled: you still have some climbing ahead. At 1.5 miles you emerge onto a small area of open rock offering some views.

At 2.3 miles you come to a junction with the Ranney Trail, which starts in Keene Valley. From this junction it's 0.9 miles to the Hopkins summit (and 3.7 miles to the summit of Giant). The trail continues to climb moderately to another junction at 3.0 miles. Turn left and be prepared for a short but steep scramble, using roots and rocks for holds. Emerging from the trees onto the open rock of the summit, you enjoy an expansive vista that includes many of the High Peaks, including Giant to the southeast, the Great Range to the west, and slide-scarred Dix Mountain to the southwest. In the distant southeast you can see Vermont's Green Mountains. In season, blueberries are another reward for the climb.

–TW

DIRECTIONS: From the Johns Brook bridge in Keene Valley (near the Mountaineer), drive south on NY 73 for 2.3 miles. Just after crossing the bridge over the Ausable River, look for a small pull-off and small trailhead sign on the opposite side of the road. If coming from the south, the pull-off is 6.3 miles past the intersection of US 9 and NY 73.

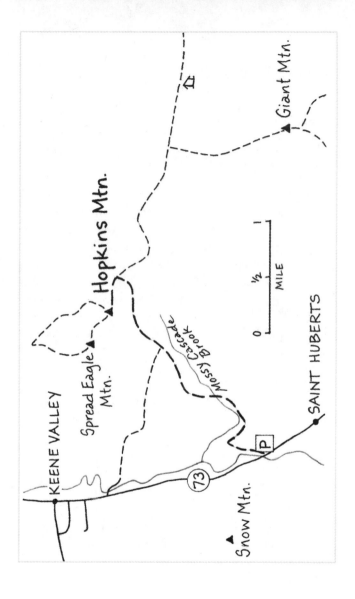

Giant Mtn.

Hopkins Mtn.

Spread Eagle Mtn.

Mossy Cascade Brook

KEENE VALLEY

SAINT HUBERTS

Snow Mtn.

73

½ MILE

0

P

4 Snow Mountain

Distance: 3.4 miles round trip
Elevation: 2,360 feet
Elevation gain: 1,360 feet
Average grade: 15.2%
Trailhead coordinates: N 44° 09.872' , W 73° 46.746'

You won't see grand vistas on the way up Snow Mountain (at least until you get to the summit), but you will encounter delightful scenes on Deer Brook of water cascading over boulders and rushing through rock flumes. You'll also pass an impressive waterfall.

> Most mountains in the High Peaks region, including Snow, are made of anorthosite, similar to the rocks found on the moon.

The beauty of the ravine makes this route to Snow preferable to the approach from the Rooster Comb trailhead near the hamlet of Keene Valley. However, the start is on private land, so hikers should not wander from the trail.

The Snow Mountain trailhead is marked by a small green sign. Begin by walking along the brook, with the water on your right. In less than a tenth of a mile, you cross a driveway. Marked by blue disks, the trail soon crosses the brook near a house and some cliffs.

As you wander upstream, the trail crosses the water several more times. Given the narrow ravine, the tall cliffs, the rugged terrain, and the constant music of the water, you

Snow Mountain looks south toward Dix and other peaks.

get the sense of being enveloped in wilderness though you are less than a half-mile from the road.

At 0.5 miles, you cross to the bank on your left and angle up the hillside, reaching a junction with an old woods road in a tenth of a mile. Turning right, you soon reach a junction with a trail on the left that leads to Lower Wolf Jaw. Continue straight, now following yellow markers.

To the right, you can still see Deer Brook as it pours over an expanse of bedrock slab. At 0.8 miles, you come to a wooden bridge over the stream. Don't cross yet! Follow a herd path along the bank for 250 feet to a large waterfall sluicing over smooth rock.

Soon after returning to cross the bridge, you come to a Forest Preserve sign at the boundary of the High Peaks Wilderness. The trail bends left, following an old tote road. At 1.1 miles, you cross a small stream where hikers have created herd paths in an effort to avoid muck.

You come to another junction at 1.2 miles. The trail on the left leads to the Ausable Club at St. Huberts. Continuing straight, you pass through a muddy patch before reaching the junction with the spur trail to Snow at 1.4 miles. Turn right.

The trail to the summit is short but steep in places. As you near the top, you traverse bedrock slabs with views behind of Rooster Comb and its cliffs. A view from a bit higher adds Big Slide and the Brothers to the picture.

At 1.7 miles, the trail skirts the actual summit and drops slightly to open ledges where a superb vista awaits. At least three destinations described in this book can be seen: Hopkins Mountain, Giant's Nubble, and Noonmark. The slides in Giant's western cirque are prominent in the east. Other High Peaks in the scene include Dix, Dial, and Nippletop in the south. The view to the west is blocked by the forested slope of Hedgehog Mountain, whence Deer Brook originates.

In high water, it might not be safe to hike along Deer Brook. When that's the case, the public is allowed to hike up Deer Brook Way, a private road that begins just south of the trailhead on Route 73. It leads in 0.6 miles to the old woods road mentioned earlier. Our advice, though, is to wait until the water subsides. The Deer Brook gorge is not to be missed.

–PB

DIRECTIONS: From the bridge over Johns Brook on NY 73 (near the Mountaineer), drive south for 2.1 miles to the bridge over Deer Brook. Park along the road on the south side of the bridge. If coming from the south, Deer Brook is reached 6.5 miles from the intersection of NY 73 and US 9.

5 Rooster Comb

Distance: 4.8 miles round trip
Elevation: 2,788 feet
Elevation gain: 1,750 feet
Average grade: 13.8%
Trailhead coordinates: N 44° 11.126', W 73° 47.212'

The Great Range is a chain of mountains stretching more than 10 miles from Keene Valley to Mount Marcy, the state's highest summit. Extreme hikers sometimes do the entire range in a day, but many more people take enjoyment in just climbing Rooster Comb, the first and smallest peak in the range.

> In 1949, Betty Woolsey scaled Rooster Comb's cliffs and established the first rock-climbing route in the Adirondacks pioneered by a woman.

The state has built an ample parking area off Route 73 just south of the Keene Valley business district. The trail, marked by yellow disks, is dedicated to Jim Goodwin, who cut a number of Adirondack trails in the 1900s.

At the outset, the trail crosses a wetland on an elevated boardwalk and comes to the register. In a tenth of a mile it reaches a junction at a small pond. Turn left here. After skirting the pond, the trail begins a steady ascent through a hemlock forest. For the most part, the grades are moderate, thanks in part to the use of switchbacks.

At 0.65 miles, you reach a junction with a trail on the left

Rooster Comb sits on the edge of the High Peaks Wilderness.

that leads to Snow Mountain, 1.8 miles away. Strong hikers might want to knock off both mountains on the same trip. However, the more scenic route to Snow, described elsewhere in this book, follows Deer Brook.

At 1.5 miles, the trail crosses a small stream. As you continue to ascend, the hemlocks give way to typical Adirondack hardwoods such as yellow birch, sugar maple, and American beech.

The trail reaches another junction at 1.85 miles next to a garage-size boulder. From here, the yellow trail goes straight toward Lower Wolf Jaw, the first High Peak (above 4,000 feet) in the Great Range. If you're going to Rooster Comb, however, you want to turn right.

Now following blue markers, the trail passes through a field of boulders, perhaps pried off the Rooster Comb cliffs during the ice age. After a couple of switchbacks, you

The Brothers and Porter Mountain can be seen to the northeast.

come to a spur trail at 2.1 miles. It leads in a tenth of a mile to a bedrock outcrop that looks down on the hamlet of Keene Valley and offers views of several other summits described in this book, including the Brothers, Little Porter, Blueberry, Hurricane, and Hopkins. The vista is well worth the short detour.

Beyond the spur, the trail continues on the level a short distance, bends sharply to the right, and comes to a wooden ladder. Soon after surmounting the ladder, you emerge from the evergreens onto the wide-open summit, with views of the High Peaks Wilderness straight ahead and of Giant Mountain behind (to the east).

—PB

DIRECTIONS: From the Johns Brook bridge in Keene Valley (near the Mountaineer), drive south on NY 73 for 0.7 miles to the Rooster Comb parking area on the right. This is a little past the Noonmark Diner. If coming from the south, the parking area is 8.0 miles past the intersection of US 9 and NY 73.

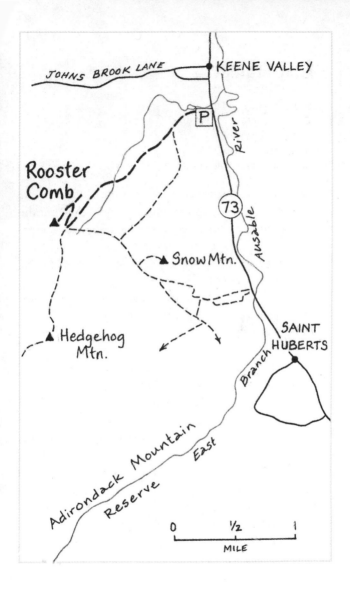

6 First Brother

Distance: 3.0 miles round trip
Elevation: 2,940 feet
Elevation gain: 1,435 feet
Average grade: 18.1%
Trailhead coordinates: N 44° 11.343', W 73° 48.944'

Hikers often take the scenic trail over the Three Brothers to reach Big Slide, one of the forty-six High Peaks, but the smaller summits are themselves worthy destinations, especially First Brother with its panoramic vista.

The hike begins at the Garden, a popular trailhead for the High Peaks Wilderness. Because the parking lot often fills up on summer weekends, the town runs a shuttle bus from Marcy Field on Saturdays, Sundays, and holidays from mid-May to mid-October.

> In 2015, an extreme athlete set a record by traversing the entire Great Range, covering 21-plus miles and climbing eight High Peaks, in 5 hours 49 minutes 38 seconds.

Two trails leave the Garden near the register. The one on the right, marked by blue disks, goes to the Brothers. At once, it begins climbing moderately, soon reaching a junction with a trail that leads to Little Porter Mountain. Continue straight.

Passing through a hemlock forest, the trail continues ascending a bit before leveling and then dipping to cross a stream at 0.4 miles. It then resumes climbing, sometimes steeply, with yellow arrows pointing the way at a few turns.

At 0.75 miles, after a brief rocky scramble, you pass a

Continuous views are the reward for hiking to First Brother.

large bedrock outcrop on the left. In just a few moments, the trail emerges onto an open ledge, where you will enjoy the first of many vistas on the way to First Brother.

Like most of the lookouts, the ledge offers a view across Johns Brook valley toward the Great Range—a chain of High Peaks culminating in Mount Marcy, the state's highest summit. From this ledge, you cannot see all of the range, but as you climb higher, the views become more expansive. To the southeast, you can see the slide-scarred cirque on the west face of Giant Mountain.

At 0.9 miles, the trail curls around a knob of bedrock, affording a view of Hurricane Mountain. Immediately afterward, you reach another spectacular vista of the Great Range. Many of the mountains have been scarred by landslides.

For the next half-mile to First Brother, it's one view after another. At times, you must scramble up bare rock, with paint blazes marking the way. Just before reaching the summit, you pass a natural shelter—a humongous boulder with a roof that sticks out like an awning.

The 2,940-foot summit, reached at 1.5 miles, affords a panorama that takes in most of the Great Range and much more, including Giant, Hurricane, Round Mountain, and the cliffs on Little Porter.

First Brother is a good place to turn around, but some may want to continue to Second Brother, which lies dead ahead less than a quarter-mile away. It, too, offers splendid views, though not in all directions. There is less reason to go all the way to Third Brother: it's about a mile from First Brother (2.5 miles from the Garden) and offers only a limited view from a single ledge. In its favor, Third's view includes the imposing cliff on Big Slide.

Of course, if you're ambitious you can hike all the way to Big Slide, which is reached four miles from the Garden. If so, you can do a loop by descending the trail along Slide Mountain Brook to Johns Brook and returning to the Garden via the Phelps Trail, which parallels Johns Brook.

—PB

DIRECTIONS: From NY 73 in the hamlet of Keene Valley, turn west onto Adirondack Street. At a T-intersection 0.25 miles after the turn, continue straight on Johns Brook Lane. Take the road to its end at the Garden, 1.5 miles from NY 73. In 2015, the parking fee was $7 per vehicle. The shuttle was charging $5 per person. To pick up the shuttle bus, drive north on NY 73 for 1.6 miles from the bridge over Johns Brook (near the Mountaineer) and turn left onto Airport Road at Marcy Field.

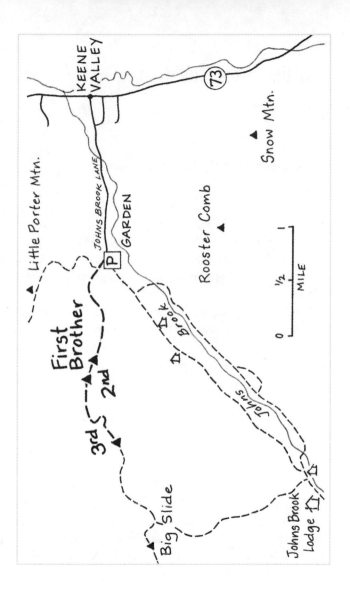

7 Little Porter Mountain

Distance: 3.8 miles round trip
Elevation: 2,745 feet
Elevation gain: 1,200 feet
Average grade: 12%
Trailhead coordinates: N 44° 11.343' W 73° 48.944'

Porter Mountain is one of the forty-six High Peaks, usually climbed from Route 73 in Cascade Pass. A longer but less-busy route starts at the Garden in Keene Valley. About halfway to Porter, the trail passes a lookout on Little Porter Mountain, a wonderful destination for those looking for a shorter excursion.

The Garden parking lot often fills up on busy weekends. To accommodate the overflow, the town operates a shuttle bus from Marcy Field on Saturdays, Sundays, and holidays from mid-May to mid-October.

Noah Porter, a president of Yale, made the first known ascent of Porter Mountain in 1875 with Ed Phelps, a local guide.

From the register, start up the trail that leads to the Brothers and Big Slide, marked by blue disks. Climbing at a moderate grade, you reach a junction at 0.2 miles. Turn right for the trail to Little Porter and Porter, now following red disks.

The trail cuts across a hillside and then turns right and descends to a sturdy bridge over lovely Slide Brook at 0.45 miles. After the crossing, the trail bears left and resumes climbing at moderate grade, passing through a stand of

Little Porter is an easy hike with a great view.

large hemlocks. Shortly, it reaches a junction with an older
trail, where an arrow directs you to bear left.

The trail soon enters private property. At 1.0 mile, you
pass a maple-sugaring shack and reach a private road. On
the other side of the road, the trail begins switchbacking up
the slope. A sign pays tribute to the late Jim Goodwin, who
laid out the first trail to Little Porter in 1924. (Goodwin's
son, Tony, is a trail builder and guidebook author.) At 1.4
miles, the trail re-enters the High Peaks Wilderness Area.

In another third of a mile, you pass a large boulder and
then follow a series of short switchbacks and stone steps
to a signpost at a junction. You've come 1.9 miles. Turn
right here to follow a short path (about 100 feet) that curls
around and emerges onto the Little Porter lookout.

The open ledges offer views in all directions. Giant

A tribute to Jim Goodwin.

Mountain, with its slide-scarred cirque, lies to the southeast. Round and Noonmark mountains are west of Giant. In the south and southwest, many of the High Peaks in the Great Range are visible, including the two Wolf Jaws, Gothics, Saddleback, and Basin. North of the Great Range, you can see the Brothers leading up to Big Slide, another High Peak, with its prominent cliff. Far below the lookout, to the east, lies the hamlet of Keene Valley.

The big cliffs north of the lookout are sometimes visited by rock climbers. Jim Goodwin put up the first climbing route on the cliffs in 1935, and his son Tony put up the second 45 years later.

—PB

DIRECTIONS: From NY 73 in the hamlet of Keene Valley, turn west onto Adirondack Street (look for the wooden sign for the Garden near the Ausable Inn). At a T-intersection 0.25 miles after the turn, continue straight on Johns Brook Lane. Take the road to its end at the Garden, 1.5 miles from NY 73. The road turns to dirt shortly before the parking area. In 2015, the parking fee was $7 per vehicle. The shuttle was charging $5 per person. To pick up the shuttle bus, drive north on NY 73 for 1.6 miles from the bridge over Johns Brook (near the Mountaineer) and turn left onto Airport Road at Marcy Field. This is the northern end of Airport Road. You pass the southern end en route.

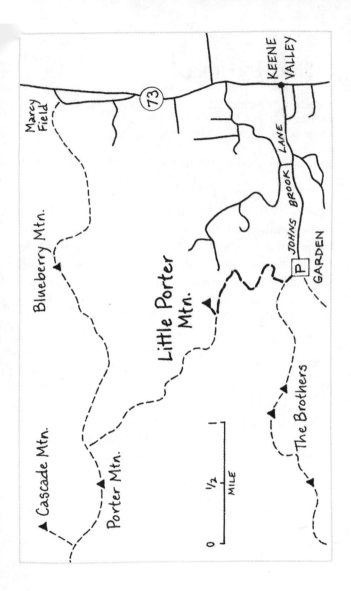

8 Blueberry Mountain

Distance: 4.8 miles round trip
Elevation: 3,050 feet
Elevation gain: 2,225 feet
Average grade: 17.9%
Trailhead coordinates: N 44° 13.118′, W 073° 47.435′

You have to work for your berries—and your views—on Blueberry Mountain. It's one of the steepest trails in this book. But those who ascend the 2.4 miles to the summit are in for a treat, and not just the sweet blue snacks of midsummer. A series of open rock slabs as you approach the summit offers a variety of expansive views. And the summit itself gives a 360-degree vantage of peaks both near (Porter and Cascade) and far (the Sentinels and Whiteface).

The steep climbs through the forest and the scrambles over open rock nearer the summit will present challenges for young children and those with physical limitations.

> Marcy Field is home to an extensive farmers market on Sundays from mid-June through mid-October.

The trail begins at the end of the parking area next to Marcy Field on Route 73 in Keene.

Start up a wide, smooth path that reaches a junction at 0.1 miles. Straight ahead is a town trail that offers a 1.1 mile lollipop loop through the forest. Take a left here for the Blueberry Mountain trail, marked with yellow disks. After ight dip, the trail begins climbing at a moderate grade ough private land. At 0.5 miles the trail crosses a small

The hamlet of Keene Valley and many High Peaks can be seen from Blueberry.

stream, which tumbles over a pretty cascade of small drops through the woods. This stream will be a companion for more than a half mile as the trail climbs along its bank.

After the crossing, the trail becomes increasingly steep. At 1.0 mile you enter the state-owned Forest Preserve, with the boundary marked by a sign and yellow blazes on the trees. Soon after this boundary the trail turns right and crosses the stream again. For the next 0.3 miles, the trail traverses a slope in a gradual climb and gives you a chance to lengthen your stride and stretch your legs.

At 1.3 miles the trail crosses a rivulet and resumes climbing steeply. At 1.5 miles you reach the first of a series of linked open area as stone slab alternates with scrub trees, berries, and grasses. The scramble up this rock is steep and the footing can be slippery where the rock is wet. The view across the valley includes Giant and the hamlet of Keene Valley at its foot.

As you ascend over the slab, views open of Dix Mountain, with its dramatic slides, and Noonmark in the foreground. Cresting a ridge you enter a clearing with views to the north and west, including of Pitchoff on the far side of Cascade Pass and Whiteface in the distance.

Leaving this clearing, the trail levels out, then dips into a col between Blueberry's eastern and western summits. Don't be fooled by the slight descent. The western summit, which is the true top at 3,050 feet, still lies ahead, 2.4 miles from the trailhead. The view from here is 360 degrees, though with Porter and Cascade looming to the west you can't see beyond those peaks. Among the landmarks that stand out are Giant, the hamlet of Keene Valley, Hurricane Mountain, and Jay Mountain.

The summit is crowned by a large boulder, a ten-by-fifteen-foot rectangle some eight feet high in the middle of the rock clearing. Hikers have piled smaller rocks against its side to commemorate their arrival at a breathtaking spot.

Beyond Blueberry's summit, the trail continues 1.7 miles to a junction with a trail from the Garden. From there, it's 0.4 miles to the summit of Porter, one of the High Peaks. When the shuttle is running, you can park at the airfield, take the bus to the Garden, hike Porter, and descend Blueberry to return to your vehicle.

–TW

DIRECTIONS: From the Johns Brook bridge in Keene Valley (near the Mountaineer), drive north on NY 73 for 1.6 miles to a sign for Marcy Field parking on the left at the intersection with Airport Road. If coming from Keene hamlet, the turn is on the right 1.0 mile past the intersection of NY 73 and NY 9N (the turn for Elizabethtown).

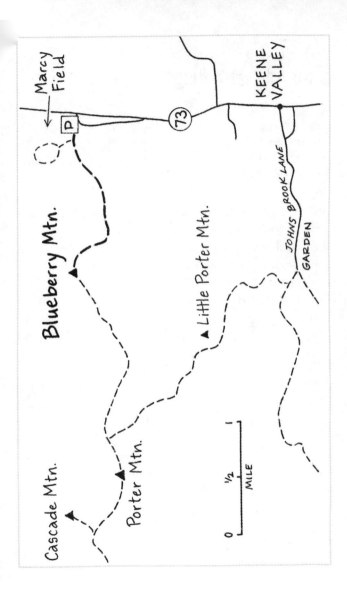

9 Nun-da-ga-o Ridge

Elevation: 3,172 feet
Distance: 6-mile loop
Elevation gain: 1,500 feet
Average grade: 8.1%
Trailhead coordinates: N 44° 15.680', W 73° 43.987'

Nun-da-ga-o Ridge in the Hurricane Mountain Wilderness has so many great views that it's impossible to count them all. The trick is not to become blasé about the scenery.

As spectacular as it is, the ridge is not for everyone. Much of the trail is not marked, though it's generally easy to follow. Also, the hike entails numerous ups and downs and in a few places scrambling up rock. Although Weston Mountain, the high point on the loop, is only 950 higher than the trailhead, with all the undulations you climb more than 1,500 feet to get there. We used this figure in calculating the grade.

> Nun-da-ga-o is reputedly derived from a Native American word meaning "Hill of the Wind." Federal maps refer to the ridge as the Soda Range.

For a much easier hike, you could just climb Big Crow, a 1.3-mile round trip. Views from this small peak are similar to those from the ridge, encompassing nearby Hurricane Mountain as well as Giant Mountain, Dix Mountain, and many other High Peaks. Other possible destinations are mentioned below.

From the parking area at Crow Clearing, start up the trail

There are numerous lookouts along Nun-da-ga-o Ridge.

(marked by red disks) that heads north toward Big Crow. After 0.2 miles, you cross a stream and begin climbing, reaching a junction at 0.4 miles. If you aren't going to Big Crow, bear right. Since the summit of Big Crow is just a quarter-mile away, many loop hikers make the side trip.

If you do opt to go to Big Crow, be sure to hike a little beyond the true summit to a broad outcrop with a spectacular view of the Great Range. You could extend the outing by continuing to Little Crow, a half-mile away on the other side of a col. This is a good option for those who aren't doing the loop as Little Crow also has nice views. If you do both Crows, the round trip is 2.4 miles.

Beyond the Big Crow junction, the Nun-da-ga-o Ridge trail is not marked. About 0.7 miles from Crow Clearing, you reach the first of many lookouts. The best vistas from the ridge are more expansive than those from Big Crow.

Also, you can find views in different directions. Although most ledges look toward the peaks previously mentioned, others offer unique vantages of Whiteface Mountain, the Jay Range, and Weston Mountain.

At 1.5 miles, the trail bends right to avoid a rock wall. Shortly after, you avoid another wall by climbing through a slot. Excluding Weston's summit, you have reached the ridge's high point. The views along this part of the ridge are fabulous. If you're not doing the entire loop, this is a good place to turn around.

The trail descends to a col, then climbs again, passing several lookouts. At 2.5 miles, you reach a wide-open ledge with views toward the High Peaks in one direction and toward the Jay Range in another. After more descent, you begin a long climb through a birch forest to the top of Weston. The summit, reached at 3.5 miles, looks down on Lost Pond and outward over countless peaks.

The descent from Weston is very steep initially. At 3.9 miles, you come to a lean-to near Lost Pond. The trail is marked again, now with yellow disks. It parallels the pond's west shore. A few herd paths lead to the water for better views. Beyond the pond, the trail descends to Gulf Brook and then returns to Crow Clearing on the level, en route passing a junction with a trail to Hurricane Mountain.

–PB

DIRECTIONS: From NY 73 in the hamlet of Keene, turn east onto Hurricane Road and drive 2.3 miles to O'Toole Lane, a dirt road. Turn left and follow O'Toole Lane for 1.1 miles to its end. This is Crow Clearing. Trails enter the clearing from the north and southeast. Be sure to find the one you want.

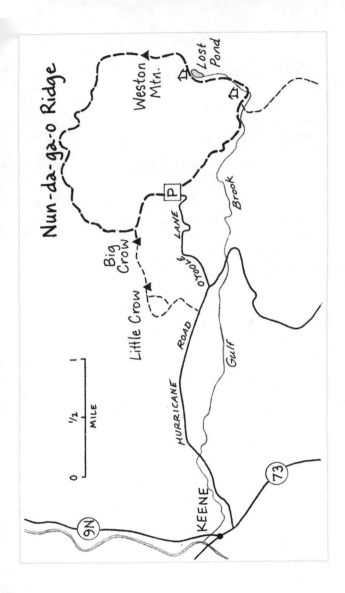

Nun-da-ga-o Ridge

Lost Pond

Weston Mtn.

Big Crow

Little Crow

P

LANE

OTOYOD

Brook

HURRICANE

ROAD

Gulf

0 ½ 1

MILE

73

9N

KEENE

10 Baxter Mountain

Distance: 2.6 miles round trip
Elevation: 2,440 feet
Elevation gain: 770 feet
Average grade: 11.2%
Trailhead coordinates: N 44° 13.239', W 073° 44.965'

Baxter Mountain offers hikers an easily accessible summit with panoramic views. There are three trails ascending this low peak, but the one from Route 9N is the easiest. It's also a joy to hike. A rerouting of the trail in 2008 used a series of long switchbacks to moderate the grade for most of the second half of the hike. Hikers encounter somewhat steep terrain only in the final third of a mile.

> Modernist master Harold Weston, one of countless artists drawn to this small peak, painted *Sunset Over Baxter Mountain* in 1920.

The summit features views of Hurricane Mountain, the Great Range, and Johns Brook valley with Mount Marcy in the distance. The hamlet of Keene Valley stands out in the lowlands below. In midsummer, wildflowers and blueberries blanket the mountaintop.

Park at a pullout on the south side of Route 9N. The small trailhead sign is set near a wooded bank and is a bit hard to see. If you are driving east and reach the intersection with Baxter Road on the right, you have gone just past the parking.

Baxter is the easiest hike, but the views are outstanding.

The trailhead sign gives a distance of 1.1 miles to the summit, but the distance to the northwest summit is 1.3 miles. The trail, marked with blue markers, passes through pine trees and crosses under a power line before beginning its gradual ascent. For the first mile it passes through private land. The trail continues over alternating level and moderate stretches before reaching the first of the switchbacks at 0.4 miles.

By traversing back and forth across the hillside, the switchbacks permit hikers to gain elevation while hardly noticing the climb. With the ascent, the forest transitions to mixed and then deciduous woods. Maple, yellow birch, and beech trees predominate here, and a relatively open understory gives the hiker pleasant views through the picturesque woods.

At 0.9 miles the trail reaches the junction with the red-marked trail from Beede Farm in Keene Valley. Continue straight, climbing moderately on switchbacks. At 0.9 miles, a rock outcropping looms fifteen feet high on the left as the trail turns right and begins to steepen and climb over waist-high ledges.

Emerging onto a clearing of open rock, you begin to see views through the trees, including a glimpse of Hurricane to the northeast. The fire tower atop Hurricane makes this peak easy to identify even by visitors who are not familiar with the landscape. And with this landmark pinpointed the observer can identify other mountains by their relationship to Hurricane on a topographical map.

From here to the summit, a number of side paths branch off, created by hikers seeking overlooks and pickers looking for blueberries, which are abundant in this area.

The trail passes the state-owned Forest Preserve boundary at 1.0 mile and reaches open rock at 1.1 miles. Here the views open to include Giant to the east and the Great Range to the southwest. Looking through the gap between Hurricane and Giant you can see the Green Mountains in Vermont.

The trail goes on to the northwest summit at 1.3 miles, which also offers wide views. The pointy peak in the foreground is Noonmark. The trail continues 1.8 miles down to a trailhead on Beede Road, making a through hike possible.

–TW

DIRECTIONS: From the Johns Brook bridge in Keene Valley (near the Mountaineer), drive north on NY 73 for 2.7 miles to the intersection with NY 9N on the right (the turn to Elizabethtown). Drive east on NY 9N for 1.9 miles to the trailhead on the right. If coming from Keene hamlet, the turn onto 9N will be on the left 1.5 miles past the local firehouse.

1 1 Hurricane Mountain

Distance: 6.6 miles
Elevation: 3,694 feet
Elevation gain: 2,040 feet
Average grade: 11.7%
Trailhead coordinates: N 44° 12.691', W 073° 43.367'

Hurricane Mountain is a regional landmark, easily recognized by its fire tower. And it's a popular hike, offering fantastic views in all directions from its open summit. There are three trails to the top, but the one from Route 9N is in exceptional shape, having been rerouted and improved in 2014. A series of plank bridges keeps hikers dry while crossing wetlands and skirting beaver ponds. At 3.3 miles, the trail is a bit longer than the old route, but the grade generally is easier on the knees.

> Hurricane's clear view of two Lake Champlain lighthouses allowed Verplanck Colvin in 1873 to establish his exact location and extend his Adirondack survey into the High Peaks.

The hike begins on the north side of Route 9N between Elizabethtown and Route 73. The trailhead sign has not kept pace with the trail improvements, still giving 2.6 miles as the distance to the summit. Marked with red disks, the trail climbs a bank from the highway, then continues at a moderate grade, reaching a stream with a small cascade on the left at 0.2 miles.

At 0.4 miles a small overlook provides a view toward

Giant Mountain, and in another 50 yards a larger rock slab creates a wider view of the same prospect. The trail levels and continues on a dry, smooth path, then at 0.7 miles reaches the first of the plank footbridges over streams and wetlands, the longest spanning close to a hundred feet. At 1.1 miles, you reach the smaller of two beaver ponds on the left. The larger is 0.2 miles farther up the trail.

Hurricane's fire tower will be preserved for posterity.

After the second pond, the trail begins to climb moderately, then increasingly steeply through a mixed hardwood forest. At 2.1 miles the trail eases and traverses the side of a hill before steepening again. At 2.7 miles you come to the first view of Hurricane's summit, with the tower poking its head above the summit rock. To the east, Lake Champlain is visible in the distance; Giant Mountain looms to the south, with Dix Mountain beyond.

The trail climbs steeply from here and at 3.0 miles reaches a junction with the trail from Crow Clearing. Bear right here. After a short dip, you begin the final ascent, scrambling over waist-high ledges and emerging onto open rock where cairns mark the route.

Walking across the open rock you can look out in every direction. Lake Champlain is again visible, with Vermont's Green Mountains beyond. In addition to Giant and the Dix Range to the south, much of the Great Range is seen extending across the southwest horizon.

This encompassing view has made Hurricane an important vantage for more than 130 years. Nineteenth-century surveyor Verplanck Colvin used the peak to take sightings of the surrounding terrain. In 1910, Hurricane became one of the first Adirondack summits used by fire watchers, and the fire tower was built in 1919. The tower went out of service in 1973 and was closed to the public. It had been targeted for demolition, but the state agreed in 2014 to let it stand. The volunteer group Friends of Hurricane Mountain Fire Tower hoped to begin restoring the structure in 2015 so it could be reopened for the public's enjoyment and education.

–TW

DIRECTIONS: From the Johns Brook bridge in Keene Valley (near the Mountaineer), drive north on NY 73 for 2.7 miles to the intersection with NY 9N on the right (the turn to Elizabethtown). Drive east on NY 9N for 3.4 miles to a parking area on the right. The trailhead is across the road. If coming from Keene hamlet, the turn onto 9N will be on the left 1.5 miles past the local firehouse.

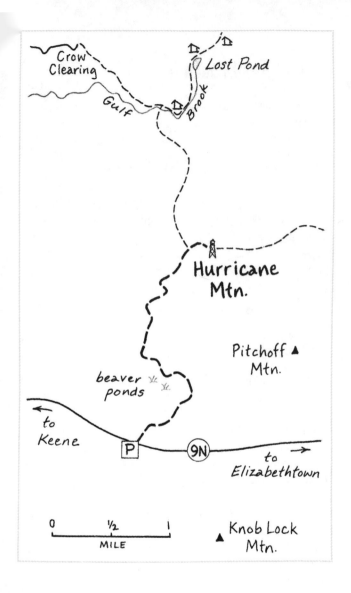

Crow Clearing

Lost Pond

Gulf

Brook

Hurricane Mtn.

Pitchoff ▲ Mtn.

beaver ponds

to Keene

P 9N

to Elizabethtown

0   ½   1
MILE

▲ Knob Lock Mtn.

12 Owl Head Lookout

Distance: 5.2 miles round trip
Elevation: 2,530 feet
Elevation gain: 1,430 feet
Average grade: 10.4%
Trailhead coordinates: N 44° 12.744', W 073° 40.736'

Poking its sharp, craggy crown above the forest blanketing the northern approach to Giant Mountain, Owl Head Lookout gives hikers a less familiar view of the Giant of the Valley and the peaks that surround it. The hike is one of the easier trips described in this book and rewards the visitor with views as special as many a higher peak. The view to the south includes the east face of Giant with its broad slide. Rocky Peak Ridge extending to the east boasts its own, smaller slides. Nestled close to Giant, Rocky Peak Ridge is also known as Giant's Wife.

> The annual Great Adirondack Trail Run begins at the Owl Head trailhead and ends in Keene Valley.

Most of the 2.6-mile trail to the lookout makes an easy-to-moderate ascent, much of it along Slide Brook, whose musical rapids provide pleasing accompaniment to the forest sounds. The final, steeper pitch to the summit is short and not an obstacle.

Don't confuse Owl Head Lookout with Owls Head, a peak in Keene that's described in the *Explorer*'s earlier guidebook, *12 Short Hikes Near Lake Placid*. The well-

Owl Head Lookout's payoff is a 270-degree vista.

marked trailhead for Owl Head Lookout is on the south side of Route 9N between Elizabethtown and Keene.

Starting at the end of the small parking area, the trail follows a dirt road for 0.1 miles, then turns off to the left, following red markers, and soon crosses a stream on a footbridge. The trail begins a steady, gradual climb through private land; the path in this early section is wide and smooth, allowing hikers to walk side by side. At 0.4 miles the trail enters the Giant Mountain Wilderness of the state-owned Forest Preserve. The grade alternates between gradual-to-moderate and level stretches.

The trail narrows to footpath width, and at 1.1 miles reaches Slide Brook, which drops into a rocky pool on the hiker's left. Crossing Slide Brook on a substantial footbridge, the trail climbs steeply up the bank, crosses a tributary stream, then ascends along the brook. The trail stays with the brook for three quarters of a mile, crossing back and forth occasionally and keeping a gentle-to-moderate grade. The mixed forest gives way to deciduous woods.

At a junction 2.5 miles from the parking area, the spur trail to Owl Head Lookout is reached on the left, marked by yellow disks. The main trail continues another 3.1 miles to a lean-to and 4.9 miles to the summit of Giant.

From the junction, the lookout trail climbs steeply for 0.2 miles to a largely open summit. From the bedrock slab, the hiker has a nearly 270-degree view dominated by Giant to the southwest, with Rocky Peak Ridge on its left and Green and Knob Lock mountains to the right. To the far right on the north stands Hurricane Mountain with its fire tower clearly visible. A path that continues a short distance into the trees beyond the slab extends the view to the east and northeast to include the Green Mountains in Vermont.

On the return hike, it's worth making a short side trip by taking a left at the junction with the Giant Mountain trail. In 0.1 miles the trail emerges into a grass and bedrock clearing. At the base of the clearing, where the trail re-enters the forest, turn around for a view of the lookout's cliffs rising above the trees. Retrace your steps for the hike back to your car.

–TW

DIRECTIONS: From the Johns Brook bridge in Keene Valley (near the Mountaineer), drive north on NY 73 for 2.7 miles to the intersection with NY 9N on the right (the turn to Elizabethtown). Drive east on NY 9N for 5.6 miles to a dirt road on the right, marked by a wooden DEC sign. Turn here and go a short distance to the parking area on the left. If coming from Keene hamlet, the turn onto 9N will be on the left 1.5 miles past the local firehouse.

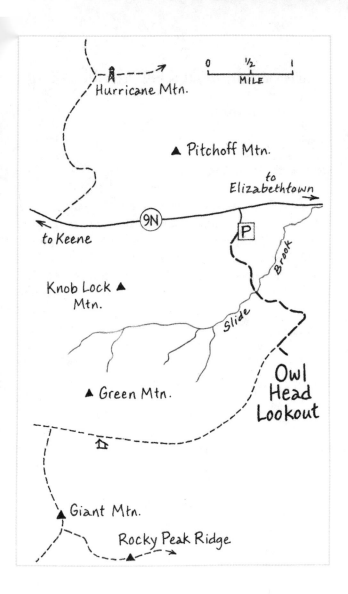

BONUS HIKE **Adirondack Mountain Reserve**

Distance: 9.9 miles round trip
Elevation: 2,700 feet
Elevation gain: 1,350 feet from gate
Average grade: 10.4%
Trailhead coordinates: N 44° 08.993', W 73° 46.069'

The Adirondack Mountain Reserve is a 7,000-acre preserve owned by the Ausable Club that encompasses Lower and Upper Ausable Lakes as well as approaches to many of the High Peaks. As part of a land deal with the state in 1978, the public is allowed to hike on trails in the AMR.

There are a number of worthy destinations within the reserve, but perhaps the best is Indian Head, a small peak with a spectacular view of Lower Ausable Lake, a finger of water walled in by mountains on either side. Impressive views also can be seen from nearby Fish Hawk Cliffs.

> **AMR RULES**
> No off-trail travel
> No camping, hunting
> or fishing
> No dogs or other pets
> No bicycles

The trails to all destinations, including Indian Head, branch off the Lake Road, a 3.5-mile dirt thoroughfare that starts near the club's main building and ends at a boathouse at the foot of Lower Ausable. Hikers are not permitted to drive on the gated road or ride the club's shuttle bus. They must park in the public lot off Ausable Road and walk a half-mile to the Lake Road.

Indian Head and Fish Hawk Cliffs can be done in

Indian Head looms above Lower Ausable Lake.

a roughly 10-mile lollipop loop that also takes in pretty flumes and cascades along Gill Brook. Although longer than other hikes in this book, most of the walking is along the Lake Road and Ausable Road.

From the parking lot, walk up Ausable Road past the golf course (with its great view of Giant Mountain) to the Lake Road. Turn left. In 0.2 miles, you reach a register and gate. After signing in, hike up the Lake Road for 3.3 miles to a height of land (beyond here the road descends to the lake). You have gained about 700 feet in elevation from the register. On the left is the trail to Indian Head.

Marked by yellow disks, the trail climbs 0.9 miles via a series of switchbacks to Indian Head, gaining another 650 feet in elevation. On the way, it passes Gothic Window, a lookout with a view of Gothics. The summit's broad ledges look straight down on Lower Ausable. Sawteeth rises directly above the lake, with much of the Great Range visible in the background. To the south you can see Nippletop and Mount Colvin, two other High Peaks.

Continue 0.2 miles on the yellow trail, passing through a col, to Fish Hawk Cliffs, where you will enjoy a dramatic view of Indian Head. In another 0.5 miles, you reach a junction with the trail to Colvin. Turn left and go 1.1 miles to return to the Lake Road. Part of this trail parallels Gill Brook. It is scenic but sometimes rough. Once back at the road, turn right. It's 1.8 miles to the register and 2.5 miles to the parking area. (On the return to the Lake Road, you pass two other trails, the first an alternate route to Indian Head, the second a short cut back to the road.)

A variety of shorter hikes are possible in the AMR. Some of the more popular destinations are shown on the map: Bear Run and Cathedral Rocks, Lost Lookout, Beaver Meadow Falls, and Rainbow Falls. All are reached via the West River Trail, which parallels the left bank of the Ausable River. The East River Trail follows the opposite bank. You can combine the two river trails in loops of varying lengths.

—PB

DIRECTIONS: From the bridge over Johns Brook (near the Mountaineer), drive south on NY 73 for 3.3 miles to Ausable Road on the right. As soon as you make the turn, you will see the public parking area on the left. (Note that this is the southern end of Ausable Road. On the way to the trailhead, you pass the northern end in St. Huberts.) If you're coming from the south, the turn will be on the left 5.3 miles past the intersection of US 9 and NY 73.

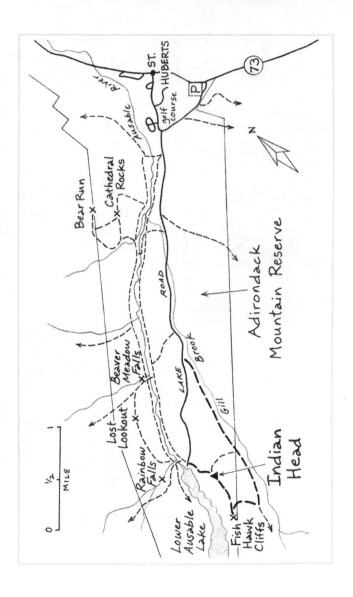

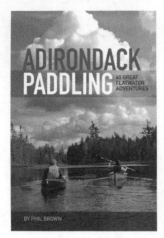
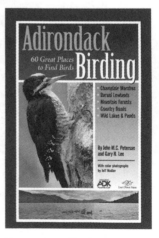

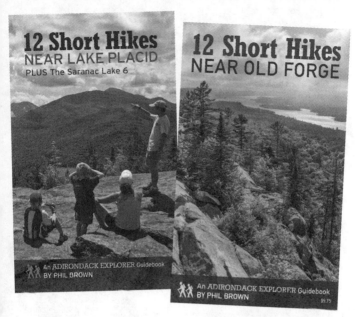

Also available!

You don't have to be a seasoned hiker or spend long days on the trail to enjoy the wonders of the Adirondacks. Phil Brown, editor of the *Adirondack Explorer*, has written two guidebooks to show you the way to low peaks, hidden waterways, and scenic overlooks near some of the Park's most popular tourist destinations.

12 Short Hikes Near Lake Placid and *12 Short Hikes Near Old Forge* are pocket-size guides to hikes that families can enjoy together in under four hours. Find them for sale in stores and at www.AdirondackExplorer.org for $9.75 each.

EXPLORE
the Adirondacks
Subscribe now and enjoy year-round adventures

THE ADIRONDACK EXPLORER

7 issues a year packed with hikes, paddles, ski treks, climbs, birding, wildlife plus all the information you need to stay on top of the issues that shape this great Park. Only $27.95 a year.

Subscribers enjoy free access to our Adventure Planner, an online collection of hundreds of excursion stories complete with photos, maps and directions.

Visit AdirondackExplorer.org for more info.
Or call 1-888-888-4970.